AF587071

# The unbecoming

## A letter to my sisters

*Unbecoming. Adjective*

1. Conduct unbecoming,

shocking or unsuitable.

Unflattering, unseemly. Not fitting,

inappropriate.

Untangling, unearthing.

2. Unbecoming who you were not.

To remember who you are.

Stripping away the expectations of others.

The rebuilding of self.

This book is dedicated to the survivors of abuse and trauma worldwide.

May you find the strength and courage needed to get out of toxic relationships, the support and strength you need to heal, and find peace. Change is coming....

Authors note.

Part poetry, part journal, and part commitment to helping others on their journey, this book wrote itself. Like a phoenix through the fire, I could look back and see the path of pain, trauma, and isolation my life went down. I truly feel like I've emerged scorched but healing and a new path lay before me. If these words help one woman to heal also, I will consider it to be a success. Women helping women rise together.

I hope these words encourage you, Love Kirsti.

Chapter 1 – This silence. Pg 11

Chapter 2 – I see you. Pg 19

Chapter 3 - The vessel. Pg 27

Chapter 4 – Grow up wild. Pg 37

Chapter 5 - There is a line. Pg 43

Chapter 6 - Patriarchy. Pg 47

Chapter 7 – The Hills. Pg 53

Chapter 8 – We did it. Pg 59

Chapter 9 – My mantra. Pg 63

Chapter 10 - My reason why. Pg 65

# Chapter 1

This silence festers. It's an infection of the heart. Maybe you need to show them your pain, or maybe you just need to stand in its way and say, no more. I won't carry this burden any longer. Either works. Just draw a line in the sand and say no more. Repeatedly, if necessary, no one is counting. Maybe your pain will cause them more too. Didn't they earn it though? By their choices, their actions, and their silence? They could have done things differently. Protected you, supported you, and listened to what you had to say. When they didn't, you tried to tell them in

other ways. You yelled, screamed, and lashed out. They heard that! Then you were "bad". A problem. And you were a problem. There must be something wrong with you. They shaped you into this yet still asked, "Why"?
Ignorant of the role they played.
Your version of events doesn't fit their pretty story. The one they cling to so tightly and tell themselves.
If they repeat it often enough it must be true? It took ages to wear you down into a quiet and compliant but unrecognizable version of yourself.
Then it became your problem though.
With no idea how to fix yourself.

It took time and practice. Did you intuitively figure it out? Find your way? Or did you stuff it down and numb your pain? Passing it along to your children and your children's children.

Turning a blind eye to the pain being passed along to the next one in line.

Sooner or later, you will hit a wall though. Your relationships suffer, and bad choices keep you in the same rut.

Until you can't take it anymore. You would rather be done than live this way.

Did you find a helping hand? Someone to talk to that helps you heal?

Feelings of hurt and pain lose their power when examined in the daylight.

They won't like it.

They couldn't get there themselves so watching you might stir them up.

That's theirs to figure out though. Not yours. They will try to make it your fault if they can. Don't let them. You erect your walls to your new home.

Build them up to hold yourself safe inside while keeping out what doesn't serve you. Boundaries protect you and just stating them out loud is magic.

The more you say it the better you feel about standing up for yourself.

The more it becomes the truth. It always was true. You stop listening to their false narrative that they tried to convince you was reality.

So, whisper with me until you can shout.

Gaze at yourself in a mirror and say,

"I love you. It's not your fault.

I am free to be who I want to be".

Who are you?

This life is yours to create.

Choose the path you want for yourself

and don't worry where it takes you.

Just walk it. Take one

step, then another, and another.

Crawl if you must, until you can walk-then

run. And say to yourself," I deserve

everything good that is

mine to have. You can't give this to

me, I have to do it for myself."

Your hands may shake. Every cell will
vibrate and feel raw. Let it. Let it all
shake out until it reaches
a pitch and resonance that melds
together. Like a cracked teacup healed
with gold, you are whole, and though you
are dented and scarred, it's ok.
Your light shines brighter through the
patina of wisdom. You are spectacular!
Let the good come to you. You deserve
it. Often one person in the family will
become the truth-teller.
The cycle breaker. The scapegoat. It feels
like punishment
until you realize how strong you are.

You are the healer. The leader who shines the way for others to follow. Forged in the fire you are tempered with resolve.

## Chapter 2

I see you. I see you shed your cloak.

The one you put on or perhaps you were dressed in along the way.

It's time to hang it up.

It never fit you in the first place.

Mine was made of guilt and shame and it kept me quiet and compliant.

Silence never helps the victims.

It's designed to keep others comfortable, not you. You were drowning in it. It hid your pain, disguised your trauma and it gave the appearance of guilt.

The weight became too much.

It was your fault you see. Words of my mother echoed in my head. I thought they

were my words but I was wrong.
Somehow, your young self must be held responsible. It couldn't be their fault, right? They didn't mean to hurt you.
You were too trusting, pretty, or unprotected. That was an invitation you see. It was just once. Or twice... and it hasn't happened again, right?
With them anyways.
"So be quiet! Why do you have to make trouble? You just want attention."
Voices from the past still sound loud in my mind. So, just keep going. Go to work.
Take care of them. Do what you are told and be quiet. Don't let your drama hurt a good person.

It wasn't a big deal!

Did you think you were the only one?

Me too.

Put down your drink, drug, or snacks. Or, maybe have another. Can I get you one?

That will make you feel better.

"I love you! You were so much trouble!

You were a difficult child.

I don't know where you get it from."

I don't deserve this... but you see - you didn't. And neither did they.

They should have protected you.

You were innocent and your light shone bright. The wrong people saw it and took a piece for their own.

Every one of them took some. It wasn't

theirs to keep. That bright light that
shines from you wasn't something they
could take, they just thought they could.
It wasn't a thing they could put
in their pocket.
It was a crack in your armor
your light shined out through.
You held those cracks open thinking they
were pieces missing but you were wrong.
Those walls became a prison over time.
You don't need that armor anymore; it
doesn't serve you.
Its weight holds you down.
It makes you keep others apart from you,
where it feels safer.
It kept out the good ones too though.

Nobody got inside and it was cold and lonely. You can seal those broken edges and cracks with love and acceptance. You can patch your dents and hold your light with loving kindness.
Let it shine freely and drop your armor.
Grow out of its rigid space and learn which people help you
grow and lift you up, and which people stay on the other side of the boundaries. you place. That is what really keeps you safe. You weren't the problem, they were.
You see, their light was stolen too.
They tried to heal their broken edges with Light stolen from you.
They were wounded along the way also.

It's not your burden to carry.
You are perfectly you.
You shine and when you give yourself
back your broken and battered edges
and let yourself shine once more
you will be free. Free to live your life in
peace. That's your gift to give.
Not to others, but to yourself.
All the inner children within you that
became frozen in time with open wounds.
Your body remembers. It shaped you in
ways you didn't understand and had no
control over. Your brain built itself new
pathways and shuts off others.
It can be healed. Hold yourself high and
let your light shine.

A tipping point is reached eventually
where the load becomes
too heavy to continue to carry and
suddenly you are at the point
where there is a choice between
the life you have led and the life you want
to lead. You can't do one more moment
living the way you have been until now.
What was your last straw?
An argument or fight? Maybe a quiet
realization in the dark of night,
tears on your pillow telling you that you
can't continue on.
Rock bottom is ok though... it's real.
Authentic. And a solid base to build
yourself back up.

## Chapter 3

You feel like the vessel. Holder of pain,
truth, and secrets. It's a burden too big to
carry forever. It's not all yours anyway,
It just rolled downhill until it got to you.
Are you the obedient one?
Doing your duty to march along with
them or are you the broken straw?
It got to be too much and released from
you like a flash flood
washing over everything in its path.
Watching them believe their own
stories about you
while you protect them from what they've
done. The knowing in their eyes while
selling pretty lies.

Laughing out loud while you
shed silent tears.
You would like to package it all up. Load
each suitcase and send them home.
Let them deal with their own mess.
You were never asked to carry it. They
assumed you would if you wanted to stay
part of their lives.
And you did. You thought the other
option was being alone or so it seemed.
You wouldn't have though. Often others
rise with you emboldened by your
courage. Sisters by choice.
Sometimes brothers too. A chosen family.
Who love you with all of your scars.
Your birth family is supposed to care for

you. Not touch you there or make you Nothing in their eyes. Look away from your anguish so they can continue to not acknowledge the truth.

Spew ugliness and rage to sway others' opinions. It's not a club you join though they tried to make it that way. Selling their version to avoid accountability. Or pretending it was different because they aren't strong enough yet to do what you have. Don't wait for them. They will follow you as they become ready. Or not. It's not on you. As a vessel being filled, you can only hold so much. The pressure of keeping the peace for holidays and

events. Don't wreck it for everyone like they wrecked you all along. "It's your burden to carry so step up!" They ignore the fact that their peace comes at the expense of yours. You are not considered. They were generous to include you after all your drama. Proud of themselves for their benevolence. It's gross. That you are only acceptable if you fold yourself into the cold little box, they've made for you.
Climb out of it.
Or kick it apart if necessary. Can I help?
Start small if you need to then
let it grow as you gain strength.
It wasn't a "misunderstanding." You aren't confused, you know. He said it was an

innocent tickle fight. The rage in his eyes
while he forced your body isn't the same
as a playfight is it?
Like a trap springing closed when the
others left. He pounced.
You know the truth and live with its
family. PTSD, mental health issues, and
self-damaging choices
moved into your being a long time ago.
It's not always like that.
Sometimes it feels like love even.
Or the promise of it.
The sweet pressure and manipulation.
Playing house while fooling you into
thinking it was everything.
Until you find yourself buried,

black and blue, with no end in sight.
Sometimes it's a numb coping tool...
Hurt them first to pretend you are in
control of what happens next.
Sometimes you play house and he's the
daddy. This is what mommies and
daddies do! But you
were a child, and he wasn't.
And he knew the truth all along.
He didn't get away unscathed either. His
spirit and soul warping and hardening.
However, it was never enough. He
deserved more. He had years to rehearse
his lies to make them
believable when you acted "crazy"
and lied to them.

Who are they going to believe?
Programmed to accept his lies at
face value, unable to face
their own pain, it's easier to stay mute.
Lines blur between all of them. Molested,
assaulted and raped over and over by
various “good” men.
Ask the "crazy" ones...they will tell you
the truth. Can you listen and hold space
for them? You were brought up to be
compliant. You "forget" so you can live.
Though it's still there whispering in your
ear in moments you let your guard down.
It haunts your dreams and guides your
choices. It comes out a little at a time
when you lower your defenses.

Unless it's pushed over the edge until a
volcano of truth spews forth scorching
everyone in its path.
"See, I told you she was crazy."
You dream of fire-filled vengeance though
it adds another wound to your heart.
Your brain plots ways to make you as ill
on the outside as you are inside.
Building new pathways to connect you to
your pain inside. That's a monumental
battle to fight after you vanquish the
dragon. You are never done though.
Hurting yourself to cause them pain
backfires every time.
They were ok with the pain they inflicted
on you from the start.

You don't understand how you are
helping them succeed.
Healing becoming a twisted path that
doctors ignore or worse, don't believe.
It starts in your brain and then becomes
pain and exhaustion.
Half-assed diagnosis that fails to blame
the trauma as the root cause and the
decades of illness that follow.
Ask women over 50, and they
will tell you. True revenge is healing.
Loving yourself enough to choose
differently. No fires to spew just quiet
whispers of encouragement and self-love
from your lips as you walk away and find
peace. Guard it with everything you have.

It is precious. They will try again, don't let them win. Each victory from choosing your peace and walking away straightens your back and fills you with resolve.

## Chapter 4

Did you grow up wild? Half feral with the
freedom of no supervision in a world
where you needed to fend for yourself.
The good old days. Go outside and play.
Don't bother me.
Mostly it was good. Sometimes it was
almost fatal. Sometimes you
just wished it was.
We built forts in trees and drank water in
the creek. Floated boats on the pools we
built by damming
up the waters. Roving bands of bicycle
gangs, we were invincible.

Skin browned in the sun and ropy
muscled, we were adventurers in the wild.
And unprotected.
So alone and vulnerable we relied on the
goodness of others to not hurt us.
Most were good, but lots weren't. Do
you know how many predators live in
your community?
If you guessed, you would be wrong.
It's a lot more. Sometimes they came with
warnings, a collective knowing that you
stayed away from that guy.
Often though it was a neighbor, uncle, or
A family friend.
"Come give Grandpa a kiss."

They were supposed to protect you.

Did they?

Not back then. In my world anyways.

Was it one time? Or a lifetime of endless

pain administered regularly.

Did you know that's not normal? You see,

once you change yourself

to cope from the first time, you

shine like a beacon to other predators.

You hide a little, look down, and hope

they don't see you, but that's what they

are looking for. Vulnerable, unprotected

and it's so easy.

They are banking on you never telling.

It worked.

Brought up believing we had no voice, no
rights, or no ability to stand up for
ourselves.
Less than in value is easily labeled.
"Respect your elders!"
We were bad. Liars.
Parents are supposed to protect children.
Communities protect each other.
The culture of silence and don't ask and
don't tell is strong though.
Stronger than the traumatized mother
with her own secrets. She cried when you
were born. She hopes it will be different
for you. It wasn't and you aren't alone.
Heal it or it becomes your child's turn.

In my mother's pain, she mourned the
loss of my innocence.
Then pushed me away because she
couldn't hold the pain.
Then blamed me, labeled me, and finally
threw me away. Like a broken vase, she
couldn't stand to look at anymore.
Knowing what I went through but
unwilling to step up or see my hurts.
I guess I thought I really was unlovable
and unworthy. It made sense at the time
to follow the path I was on.
I didn't know I had a choice.

A revolution is coming. Women have had
enough of being treated this way.
Less than. If we could only link arms and
make a stand for real change to happen.
It is a seething fire stuffed down by a
lifetime of unfair treatment.
It's coming though. I hope it's soon.
I hope we survive it.

## Chapter 5

There is a line dividing us vs them.

Be quiet and small. Polite and

smile for them.

"You need me but I don't need you. Be

grateful for what you have.

You can't make it without me. Accept

your lot in life, it could be worse!"

They spew lie after lie with pretend

patience at your deemed misbehavior.

Promise to change but not really...

" I just need you to stop complaining! “

“After all I do for you. So ungrateful."" I

hate it when you manipulate me

with your tears." "Ungrateful bitch.”

"I made this possible for you, and I can take it away anytime.

Where will you be then!"

Why would they change? They are running a double play.

The one they sell you that you agreed to and want, unknowing the deal you've made, and the one they secretly are doing undercover. It's out in the open though, the cover is your veil. Your hope and belief that it will get better. It's a great thing to be them and in charge.

Thinly veiled misogynists and narcissists.
Dinosaurs in the flesh refusing to evolve.
"You are worth less than I am and must
work harder to make up for it."
Contribute more, take care of everyone
and everything, and don't ask for more.
This yoke of servitude and compliance is
voluntary to put on
yet who told us we could choose better?
Trained from birth to be less. Expect less.
There is an army of women who are
done. We don't comply.
We are not being quiet any longer either.
Arm and arm we will call it out.
We will tell the truth and lift our sisters.

Together we rise and the world will be changed. And good men will rise to meet us.

The old systems don't fit them either. Good men exist. We know some of them and love them. The problem is their silence in the face of our vulnerability. We need you to stand for us.

Speak up. If it's only 1 out of ten men that are abusive, but the other 9 do nothing they are part of the problem. Looking away from the misdeeds of their brothers. It's not all men, but it is all women. Ask them, they all have stories.

## Chapter 6

Patriarchy. The line that divides us is not

just men vs women though...

It's also the unevolved, the pain-filled

pushing us down and the silent

or weak voice avoiding conflict.

Men hurt men too. And boys.

Our treatment is too difficult for them to

bear witness to.

Their angry dismissiveness tells us to "be

quiet and grateful".

"You need me, I don't need you". "You

Are nothing without me".

"You must accept your lot in life.

You lost the genetic roulette game but

that's not on me".

"It could be worse"! "You are worth less
than me, so you have to do more"
"Never my equal no matter how hard you
try. That's just the way it is."
"What are you complaining about?"
"Fine, I'll agree to change"
(But I won't really....)
"I just need you to stop." "Stop nagging
me". "I hate when you manipulate
me with tears". "I made this possible for
you, so don't forget it!" This yoke of
servitude and compliance is voluntary to
wear...but nobody told us that.
I won't comply.
And I'll help free you from yours too.

The men in my life who broke me piece
by piece were community leaders,
neighbors, relatives, and
partners. They were rarely strangers...
They looked trustworthy. Safe.
If the true number of them were revealed
it would be shocking and likely
labeled a lie. It couldn't be true, can it?
It is. When you are raised in a broken
system, broken people look
familiar. They are somewhat predictable.
The battle within oneself to heal
and make better choices is a
marathon many never complete.
If patriarchy is a castle, we are the
foundation of the steps.

They climb on us and over us to rise to
the heights they seek.
Those steps are crumbling so men build
ladders. The steps are ignored, eyes
shying away from seeing. They couldn't
get there without us.
Every man on earth is born of a woman
who made his life possible.
As women, we need to help
each other up also.
Men are lucky women only want equality,
not revenge. All we ask is to be left alone
and have the same options and choices
men do. Why is that so hard to
understand? Or even an option to deny
us? They refuse to change, forcing us

down. Angry at being left behind in the
evolutionary race and
rage-filled at our arrogance and
ignorance. Vilified, molested, and killed in
horrifyingly large numbers
deemed acceptable.
They shrug at our rage.

## Chapter 7

The hills before me.

I see now how parents are supposed to protect their children.

Seeing my son walking off into the night with the pedophile who has haunted me since childhood broke something inside me. He was ok, nothing happened, but I wasn't. We were at a family gathering and nobody said anything or were even concerned in the slightest.

They were silent in their programmed state of compliance. Heads down and eyes averted. Silently hoping nothing would happen or that if it did it wouldn't bring conflict into their lives. After that night I knew they wouldn’t protect him. It was up to me. After all, they weren’t very bothered by my abuse and stuffed down their own in order to be functional. All children inside trying to hide from the boogeyman. How do you raise a new generation of good men in the company of some truly bad ones? They aren't all bad, but they are all silent which isn't much better. Not strong enough to confront the truth, they look away to get along. Growing up in a safe and protected environment with unconditional love and the expectation of doing the right thing even when it's hard has allowed my son to be the kind of man I'm proud to be raising. Knowing I needed to keep him away from family so he could be this man is heartbreaking but worth the pain it caused us along the way. Necessary. Our circle is now smaller but it's authentic and safe. I came back after a long absence I needed, to find myself and unbecome everything I wasn't with the hopes of building bridges with family. I realized that even though I spent many years healing myself, they didn't. They didn't hit rock bottom and break into a better version of themselves with work, support, and time to heal.

They were numb to the pain and expected me to fit back into the little space that was left vacant when I went away the last time. The problem is I can't and won't. Stuff it down, smile through the pain, pretend to belong.

Be respectful and polite to monsters with gloating eyes. I reject my membership in their club. Unhealed trauma rolls downhill to the next generation. I will be the wall that stops it. I can look back now at the alcohol and drug addiction, codependency, abuse, mental health issues, and unhealthy life choices that have plagued my family for generations. We were dubbed "the crazy ones",

the ones who left, or
broken into messy pieces held
together with denial and band-aids.
Who was really crazy though?
We learned to pacify, protect, and keep
our abusers comfortable.
Victims were labeled and then rejected.
How did they make this ok in
their hearts?
I'm done though. I'm hanging up my cloak
of shame and compliance.
I will no longer ignore bad behavior from
anyone and will not hope for the best.
That's not good enough anymore. The
hills rise before me but seem protective
and manageable. No longer

insurmountable mountains.
Never-ending pain stuffed down with a polite but vacant smile.
The company that meet me there on my journey or rise with me emboldened by examples are welcome. We all travel on our journey of unbecoming what we are not, then becoming what we are meant to be at our own pace.
Look around and see whose company you are in. You only felt alone. You are one among many. From where we stand there are paths open to us that weren't visible until now. Where will you go with such freedom?We rise together and the view is spectacular up here.

## Chapter 8

We did it. A seemingly insurmountable
climb from depths where no
light shines through.
Shedding layers like scales as
we grew and stretched.
Gaining clarity while finding peace. Young
ghosts who beg to be heard,
felt, and loved.
Raging quietly until we do. Our eyes
newly opened to see the lonely path that
led us here.
Voices whispering "you can't" in our ears.
Silenced by a steady heart saying
you must. Just try.
We reached a plateau of hope and

possibilities. With many paths before us
to choose from.
The pain tempered us without hardening
our hearts and swaying gently in the wind
following the
storms, we grew stronger rather than
broken.

## My Mantras

I'm done pretending to fit in their box so I can be part of family events.

I'm done seeking approval or trying to be liked.

I will no longer ignore bad behavior and hope they will change.

I can't tolerate disrespect and I will not try to raise a good man in an environment where few are.

I have healed my hurts and moved on.

I do not need to forgive unforgivable things. I can just close that door and walk forward in peace.

I will live and care for my body and my spirit who remained strong under the mountain of wounds meant to snuff out my light.

It's my turn.

## My reasons why.

My treasure warms my skin,
under sunshine and water
gliding along the bottom sleek
and free. It has young arms
around me with sticky kisses
begging to be held. A warm,
whiskery snuffle with hooves
rimmed in steel asking to fly
with me down meadows. It
tastes like flavors savoured on
my tongue in cafes with foreign
sounds in new places and
strokes on a canvas waiting to
be revealed. Clarity, resonance,
and truth. Freedom to choose
my own kind of treasure. Held
in arms secure, my home. In joy
and peace. Free

**About the author.**

Kirsti Hrist is a pen name used to protect the author's identity. Enduring decades of abuse and struggling to find peace, safety, and freedom, Kirsti hopes to encourage other survivors into healing their own traumas.

This book is not intended to replace therapy or other treatment options, but rather encourage and support the reader's own journey.

Hrist is a Valkyrie in Norse mythology and means divine wrath.

www.ingramcontent.com/pod-product-compliance
Lightning Source LLC
La Vergne TN
LVHW010120170826
845678LV00012B/2509
* 9 7 8 1 7 3 8 3 8 9 5 0 6 *